PLAN YOUR MOST SUCCESSFUL YEAR EVER!

THE STEP-BY-STEP GUIDE & YEARLY PLANNER DESIGNED
SPECIFICALLY FOR WOMEN

Design & layout: Gwyneth Wint

Publisher: Gwyneth Wint

Copyright   © Gwyneth Wint, 2011

Language: English

Country: United Kingdom

ISBN: 978-1-4709-4770-5

Revised   November 2011

Website   www.planyouryear.com

                      www.successisyours.co.uk

Important Notice

"Step inside, together we'll explore opportunities and open doorways to a new life where your action follows passion, where you live fully and choose happy"

"There's happiness in every situation, just find the funny, engage your laughter and spread the humour"

CONTENTS

If you want a purposeful life then..... make it happen…. create the opportunities… take action be passionate, live fully and get happy.

CALENDAR OF INTENT

FOR THE YEAR _____

What infinite possibilities wait in the year ahead? What do you intend to create this year? How do you intend for the year to end? Answer those questions in the space below and use the following pages to set quick goals.

January

What do you intend to accomplish?

February

What do you intend to accomplish?

March

What do you intend to accomplish?

APRIL

What do you intend to accomplish?

MAY

What do you intend to accomplish?

JUNE

What do you intend to accomplish?

July

What do you intend to accomplish?

August

What do you intend to accomplish?

September

What do you intend to accomplish?

OCTOBER

What do you intend to accomplish?

NOVEMBER

What do you intend to accomplish?

DECEMBER

What do you intend to accomplish?

NOTES

Notes

Is your life engaging? Is it enjoyable?

Are you longing for real purpose?

Could you be its creator?

ABOUT

This book is intended to help you refine your purpose, goals and aspirations. It is one of a series consisting of the following:

- A planner

- A handbook of grassroots philosophy

- A workbook

- A notepad

- A journal

- Little books of inspiration

These books are designed as personal development tools; they complement each other, yet any book can be used alone.

To find out more, turn to page 181

INTRODUCTION

Do you sometimes question your purpose in life and struggle to find meaning and value in your work and social life?

Many of our greatest and most inspiring leaders male and female, grappled with the same dilemma prior to transforming their ideas in order to bring about monumental changes with global impact.

Are you aware of the contribution you could make to this world? Do you realise that just by taking action on your ideas and following your dreams, your life has real significance for others as well as yourself?

This book is designed for you if you recognise you are capable of more than your life seems to offer yet for one reason or another, you have not found the time or energy to shape the life you would prefer to live.

Are you ready to make a change?

This planner is also for you if you already have ideas and are engaged in a project that is underway. It can assist by helping to clarify what you are aiming to achieve, focusing your ideas and you can apply the questions to specific projects. You might also be interested in the Planner Companion, which contains less text with more pages for planning. See page 181.

Ideally, your planning would commence by the latter quarter of the year prior to the initiation of your project but whenever you begin, it is always great to get started.

You begin by noting important dates for the year then reflect on the past and look ahead to the future, visualising your life as you would like it to be. You move on to de-cluttering your space as well as your mind. You will then look at SMART goal setting before writing a Statement of Intent. Next you plot the progress of your ideas and record your achievements throughout the year. There are pages for personal notes scattered throughout the planner.

Your monthly reviews support you over a period of time in seeing where you might be getting stuck. They also assist you in recognising your unique abilities and considering how you might use your talents to fulfil your life.

If at any point you remain uncertain of your ideas or what steps to take, do the following:

- Re-read your Calendar and Statement of Intent.

- Research your interest (use the Web, books, your library).

- Look at the activities you want to try.

- Choose two of the most significant.

- Put provisional completion dates in the calendar.

- Make a list of the people you need to contact in order to get started and the resources needed.

The following is an example of a simple planning process you have used many times before in different ways.

What do you do when you decide to take a vacation? You do the following:

- You think about where you dream of going perhaps making a list of destinations.

- You research the destinations, flights, hotels etc.

- You figure out how to pay for it, perhaps setting up a standing order to deduct a certain amount of money that goes into a savings account solely for your vacation.

- If you don't have enough money to travel abroad perhaps you consider something closer to home, maybe you opt for a weekend break.

- You pick a date.

- You book those days off in your diary

- You book those days off at work.

If you find it difficult getting your ideas out of your head and onto paper or computer, consider that even a lack of inspiration can provide you with useful information. It could be an indication of the following:

- That it is time to furnish your own ideas with value.

- That it is time to rise to the challenge of just being you and investing in yourself.

- That it may be time to make yourself fully aware of what goes on around you, becoming in the process, well informed about the social and political issues of the day, and educated in the things that interest you the most.

Everything you see around you was once just an idea. Your daydreams are the seeds of future creations, be they a career change, new product lines, relationships, events, empires. Big or small, ideas create reality and underpin your emotional and spiritual development. In recognising their value, ensure the thoughts and ideas you entertain, are of the highest calibre. Refuse to entertain negative beliefs about yourself. Challenge every thought that would put you down.

Do the people around you appear indifferent in the face of your enthusiasm? Do they display a lack of faith in you and your ideas? Then believe in yourself, understand the power of your own thoughts and subsequent actions.

If you would like assistance, the books *"Shaping Your Life from the Inside Out"* and *"The Handbook of Grassroots Philosophy"* (described on page 181), provide a systematic approach to help you recognise and eradicate limiting beliefs.

Spend as little or as much time on your planning activities as you see fit, just don't make that brilliant idea become another uncompleted task that adds to your anxiety. If you only have 5 minutes when you open your eyes in the morning or 15 minutes before you go to sleep at night with only one paragraph to write, that's better than nothing at all. The smallest time commitment moves you in the direction of your new life and is your first step in replacing a habit of procrastination, with an inclination towards positive action. The more time you commit to this, the more you will want to do it.

Allow yourself breathing space and listen to feedback. Very soon the answers to your questions will surface. If you have been very relaxed about things, just going with the flow, then it is time for you to take positive steps towards fulfilling an idea.

What you write in this book are the seeds of your creativity, and an expression of your heart's desire. Open up to the process of putting pen to paper and allowing yourself to be inspired, even dazzled by your brilliance and the extent of your creative thought.

Let's begin

How can you increase the pleasure and reduce the sacrifice in achieving your goals?

Here's a tip! Make a point of not missing out on important anniversaries.

IMPORTANT DATES

Remember, when you get to the destination, it is far sweeter to be embraced by those you love. Use the following pages to note important dates in the year.

January - March

	Birthdays	Anniversaries & Special Dates
January		
February		
March		

APRIL - JUNE

	BIRTHDAYS	ANNIVERSARIES & SPECIAL DATES
APRIL		
MAY		
JUNE		

27

JULY - SEPTEMBER

	BIRTHDAYS	ANNIVERSARIES & SPECIAL DATES
JULY		
AUGUST		
SEPTEMBER		

OCTOBER - DECEMBER

	BIRTHDAYS	ANNIVERSARIES & SPECIAL DATES
OCTOBER		
NOVEMBER		
DECEMBER		

NOTES

Be creative...
be brilliant... be
flexible... be
yourself.... Most
of all... be
happy.

Do what you enjoy or start enjoying what you do!

REFLECT

Use the following pages to help you examine and assess where you are in your life, where you have been and what you would like to happen next.

TAKE A MOMENT

"In stillness you plant the seeds of your creativity"

Stillness and quiet, solitude and rest, are vitally important to your development. A frenetic life leaves no time for contemplation, for renewal, or for occasion to nurture and create real change. In the turbulence of a busy life, all you can do is paper over the cracks.

Do not be afraid of inactivity. These moments of quiet, harness dynamic and powerful forces of creative energy to help bring your ideas to life. When you have rested your body and nurtured your ideas, it is then time to take action, for without decisive and co-ordinated effort, you cannot achieve success.

Take a minute to reflect on where you are in your life. Do you feel a sense of fulfilment? Or are you still waiting for your life to begin?

GO EASY ON YOURSELF

"Try to appreciate the good, the bad and the ugly"

Although life will take you in unexpected directions, you are perfectly equipped to take on the important and very significant steps required to shape the outcome of your future.

Do you believe that?

Could you consider that you could learn and that life itself teaches you all you need to know?

Any change can feel scary, but with a commitment to act from your personal best and a little bit of courage, you can do it. You have what it takes to change your life.

Do not waste valuable mental energy beating yourself up about what you have not done or where you might have failed in the past. Mistakes provide you with information. Every mistake is a lesson learned, so go easy on you.

IT IS OK TO BE YOU

"Your task is to be the best you can at being you"

Remember the following, even better, write the list out, put it in a place you regularly see, and use it as a reminder to work hard but lighten up and play a little.

- If it is not life threatening then it is OK to make a mistake, just learn from it.

- Do not "try to do" just "do it or don't". Do what you say or don't do it but make a commitment one way or the other.

- What's the worst that could happen?

- What's right about things just as they are?

- Know your own limits, but don't be limited by them.

- Determine for yourself what success means for any task you undertake. Decide what outcome you want and how you will know that you have been successful. Money is an important factor but it isn't just about money. It is wise to consider other measures of success as the financial considerations may not be the achievement that actually makes your heart sing.

- Do not belittle yourself!

As you set about your tasks, remember that your goals are mere pointers to your success, you are allowed to change your mind.

LOOKING BACK

Write about your successes. This can be any kind of success, big or small, how did it happen?

LOOKING AHEAD

What would you like to be doing 3 months from now?

Imagine you 12 months from now. Where are you? What are you doing?

Five Years Ahead

Imagine you 5 years on with skills and abilities you acquired along the way, what are you doing?

(If you find this a useful exercise then the two books *'Life Goals'* and *'Looking Ahead to the Next Five Years'* may also interest you, see page 181).

Notes

SMALL STEPS

Knowing the direction best suited for your life, happens only after you take your first tentative steps towards fulfilling your brightest ideas. The more committed you are, the clearer your vision. Think about how much time is required and how you can find it. Consider whether or not your project necessitates assistance or additional funds and how you can gather that together.

Don't let anything that's unnecessary, petty or irrelevant stand in your way. Don't give up. Recognise that obstacles often require new ways of looking at things and perhaps a different approach.

The following pages will help you in clearing away the cobwebs and gaining focus.

A BIT OF WHAT YOU FANCY

Take a few minutes to think about things you have even remotely considered trying and make a note below.

BEING

SEEING

DOING

EXPAND YOUR IDEAS

Use the space below to expand your ideas. What appeals to you the most?

THIS YEAR

Review your list of fancies and select the two for which you are most passionate. Write what they are in the space below and say why.

PASSION LIST

What activities and ideas excite you the most?

PASSION INTO ACTION

Select one activity from your Passion List. Are you ready to make it happen?

ACTIVITY	WHEN

DE-CLUTTER YOUR SPACE

Take a minute to look around your home, room, studio or office and make a note of your outstanding and uncompleted tasks.

The purpose of this is not to send you guilt tripping about what you haven't done, but to help you distinguish between the tasks that are important and worthy of being prioritised, and those that you can delegate to somebody else or to the bin.

This exercise helps free your mind so that you can focus your energy on the things you feel really inspired to do.

You may be an excellent and methodical housekeeper, fastidious in your cleaning methods; however, if you are engaged in any kind of creative process, chances are you will notice your home becoming increasingly cluttered. This de-cluttering exercise is not a one-time activity but something you will need to periodically revisit.

DE-CLUTTER LIST

THROW OUT

GIVE AWAY

DELEGATE

T ASK REVIEW

Using your lists from previous pages, add each task to one of the columns below as a task you do yourself, a task to discard or a task you would like to delegate to somebody else be it a member of your family, a business professional or a friend. Bear in mind that just because you have the skill to do something, doesn't necessarily mean you should be the person to do it.

TO DO

DISCARD

DELEGATE

Task review

To do

Discard

\

Delegate

Unblock Your Mind

If you have doubts about your goals, use the table below to help clarify your thoughts. This form of questioning based on the work of French philosopher Rene Descartes, helps the mind reveal ideas you may not normally think of.

Unblock Your Mind Exercise A

What are the positive outcomes for you of achieving your goals?	What might you be required to give up or little pleasures forego in order to achieve your goals?

UNBLOCK YOUR MIND EXERCISE B

What would happen if you carry on doing what you do now?	What opportunities will you miss out on if you don't do what you say?

What pain might you experience in not achieving your goal?

NOTES

Notes

PLAN FOR SUCCESS

What would you say about your ability to plan and put your plans into action? (Write your answer below)

Use the following pages to set simple tasks you can easily complete. It may surprise you how quickly these simple steps lead to big achievements. These tasks are not set in stone, you can change your mind at any time but it is important to make a commitment and a big effort to see them through.

Do it on purpose

Planning is not meant to replace the freedom or enjoyment of a life that flows naturally without the need for plotting every curve, however, you cannot achieve high levels of success without focus, discipline and action.

The purpose of a plan is to help you direct your thoughts towards your goals, shaping your mind and creating space in your head for new ideas. It frees you from the tyranny of constant chores and the need to engage in activities that do little to move your life forward.

It is true that there are many things in life outside your control and the best-laid plans can go awry, however, an action plan gives focus and clarity to your thoughts.

There will be times when you have important deadlines to meet and the only way to pull it off is to be disciplined in your approach, nevertheless, don't hold to rigid routines that make you unhappy. This is your life and as such, it is essential that you be present in it, having fun and living each and every day in the best way you can.

Whenever you feel overwhelmed by the thought of undertaking or completing a task, focus all your attention on a single activity and make this your priority. Forget other concerns for a moment don't worry whether or not you will be able to complete other tasks, you can go back and pick them up afterwards if you still consider them worthwhile.

How do you know when you are overwhelmed?

Look for the following:

- Tiredness at the thought of having to complete the task.

- Constantly avoiding it or putting it off.

- Feelings of frustration.

- Feeling that you have no control.

- Feelings of anger or anxiety.

The signs listed above tell you it is time to either:

- Take a step back and review whether or not you really want what you say you want.

- Consider if this thing you 'want' to achieve is really a sign of some other unmet need or desire.

- Slow down and ask for help.

DON'T WASTE YOUR ENERGY

Do not waste your energy trying to do something you really are not interested in doing or being someone who doesn't truly reflect the authentic you. If you are asked to carry out a task that you feel reluctant to undertake, rather than tying up your time trying to please somebody and then having no energy to bring your own ideas to life, hesitate before responding. Wait for a minute, an hour, a day or a week, in the meanwhile ask yourself the following questions:

- What feels right?

- Do you feel able to accomplish what is being asked of you?

- Is it worth it?

It could be that the outcome interests you, but right now is not the right time. If what you have been asked to do is a sound goal for you, then commit to it, otherwise make it known that you are not interested. Do not waste yours and other peoples' time. Make a decision and make the decision known. Remember that the most successful people are usually the most decisive and the quickest to respond.

Ask the Right Questions

If you find yourself spending a lot of time in frantic activity that doesn't really take you anywhere, stop what you are doing and start asking questions. Begin with asking questions that create opportunities rather than shut things down.

You could find yourself in the middle of an old pattern before you become fully aware of what's happening. That's okay, just correct it. Be aware each time it occurs and remind yourself to not identify with and own any negative thoughts and feelings that arise as a result of choosing you.

As an adult, there are no 'shoulds', there are choices. If you are involved in a project and find yourself having doubts about remaining part of it, ask yourself the following questions:

- What doubts do you have?

- What are the intrinsic benefits?

- How might the situation be improved?

- Are you being respected and validated for your time and knowledge? If not, are you being compensated in a way that is meaningful to you?

- What would you consider adequate compensation?

- Has enough thought gone into the project or are you just working with blind faith?

- Is this really what you want to or have you ended up here as a result of a conditioned response?

- What would you really like to be doing with your time?

Smart Goals

SMART has become an acronym for a systematic and highly successful method of setting goals. It stands for

- Specific

  Do not try to do everything at once, focus your aims.

- Measurable

  Decide what you will see at the end to show you and others the measure of your success, it could be something tangible or an experience.

- Attainable

  Despite your personal constraints and other factors outside your control, be certain that you can bring the ideas, resources and people together to achieve your goal or have the resource to bring in others who can make it happen.

- Relevant/Realistic

  Ensure your goal is not just a 'pie in the sky' idea, those involved have a connection to it and it is realistically achievable. Don't go jumping off a building without a harness to see if you can fly.

- Timely

  Give your goal a start and an end date and make sure the tasks can be completed within the timeframe allocated.

A goal that is too broad may lead you to believe it is unattainable, hence one of the key aspects of setting SMART goals is that they are very specific and the tasks can be broken down into small achievable steps.

With SMART goals you decide from the very beginning how you will know at the end, whether or not you were successful in achieving your goals. This is called your 'measure of success' It is an outcome that has meaning to both you and the other people involved and equates to the things you can actually touch, see, hold, smell or experience.

As in life, your plans may not always follow a straight path and if things do not go according to plan, the measure you previously determined will inform you of whether or not you achieved your goals. It gives you a way of quantifying the success and managing everyone's expectations.

Your goals should be realistic and attainable within a certain timeframe and also be feasible given other constraints within which you have to operate. For example, if you are pregnant it is unrealistic for you to plan to learn how to skydive during your pregnancy. If you are 60 years of age, no matter how fit you are it is highly unlikely that you would gain entry to compete in the Olympics against much younger athletes but there may be other competitive events that you could enter.

We all want to feel good about ourselves. We do things to make ourselves happy and do not want to wait too long to experience it. If we have to delay gratification, we want to know how long we will have to wait. A goal without an end date can quickly lose momentum as people get bored and lose interest or feel burdened. It is important therefore, to set a date by which you expect to complete your tasks and finally achieve your goals.

Your goals need not be about work objectives.

- Do you have a long held dream that has never been fulfilled?

- Do you wish to improve a particular relationship, or let go of one?

- Are you hoping to meet a soul mate?

- Do you long to start a family?

- Do you need to rid yourself of an addiction?

- Could you just want to make more responsible choices?

If you are experiencing uncertainty you may find it helpful to ask yourself the following questions:

- Does it suit you?

- Can you complete it without help? If not, what help do you require?

- Who can you rely on for help?

- What resistance do you have to the idea?

- What resources do you require?

Statement of Intent

To be successful you have to raise your head above the parapet, put yourself in a position of accountability and allow yourself to be seen and scrutinised. You may even be criticised, however, you are also quite likely to be criticised if you do nothing. You may find that it is the least productive people who criticise the most as they have little idea of what it takes to move an idea from mere thought into physical reality.

This is your life so make a choice about what you do with it. If someone else decides for you there's little point in blaming them if things don't quite work out the way you expected. If you do not allow your voice to be heard, if you do not speak up, you remain on the decision making team but give away your power and may have settled for less than you are worth.

Naturally decisions are made in consultation with the people who share your life and perhaps due to family commitments or poor health there are limits on the things you are able to do but there are always a number of choices you can make within those constraints. The responsibility for life ultimately rests with you.

Use the following pages to help you create a statement of intent describing what you would like your life to look like and what you would be doing in the next 3-5 years if you could go anywhere, do anything, be introduced to anyone you ever wanted to meet.

What changes would you like to see this year?

Which aspects of your personality would you like to explore this year?

What legacy would you leave behind?

STATEMENT OF INTENT

Write your statement of intent. This year I intend......

WHAT COULD YOU DO TODAY?

What could you start doing today, this week to demonstrate your ability to do, be or have the things you describe and take you closer to your dream?

QUICK GOALS

JANUARY	FEBRUARY
MARCH	APRIL
MAY	JUNE

Quick goals

JULY	AUGUST
SEPTEMBER	OCTOBER
NOVEMBER	DECEMBER

Notes

FROM DAY-DREAM TO REALITY

Use the following section to set quick goals that will motivate and keep you on track throughout the year. Do not try to cram your diary full of goals, select one maybe two goals for the year then list the small steps you need to take each month in order to fulfil those goals.

JANUARY - FEBRUARY

JANUARY

FEBRUARY

MARCH - APRIL

MARCH

APRIL

MAY - JUNE

MAY

JUNE

JULY - AUGUST

JULY

AUGUST

SEPTEMBER - OCTOBER

SEPTEMBER

OCTOBER

NOVEMBER - DECEMBER

NOVEMBER

DECEMBER

NOTES

RECORD YOUR PROGRESS

The following section provides an opportunity to plan each month in more detail and monitor your progress.

Remind yourself of your goals by writing them out each month in the space provided; doing so helps commit them to memory so they become part of your normal thinking. The stronger the idea in your mind, the easier it becomes to achieve your goals. In fact, there will be no stopping you.

On your review pages, make a record of the thoughts and emotions you experience as you set about accomplishing your tasks. Record the highs and the lows, the frustrations and the successes, as well as your new ideas and how you feel about the tasks you did not complete.

JANUARY

A plan is an effective tool when changing your life

REVIEW

What are your thoughts and feelings about this month?

What did you do this month for fun and inspiration?

Intentions and Goals

What are your intentions for the future?

What single task will take you one step closer to your dream?

OUTSTANDING TASKS

LIST OF POSSIBILITIES

Commit to your goals...

If at first you don't succeed, consider the possibility of trying again.

What do you have to lose?

FEBRUARY

Give yourself permission to make mistakes

REVIEW

What are your thoughts and feelings about this month?

What did you do this month for fun and inspiration?

INTENTIONS AND GOALS

What are your intentions for the future?

What single task will take you one step closer to your dream?

OUTSTANDING TASKS

LIST OF POSSIBILITIES

Focus on the present....

Let tomorrow unfold in your actions today. You can do nothing to speed the arrival of a new day but you can make yourself miserable waiting for tomorrow to never arrive!

MARCH

If necessary, start again!

REVIEW

What are your thoughts and feelings about this month?

What did you do this month for fun and inspiration?

Intentions and Goals

What are your intentions for the future?

What single task will take you one step closer to your dream?

OUTSTANDING TASKS

LIST OF POSSIBILITIES

Don't sit waiting for someone to come along and bring excitement to your life.

Make a start, get excited about something!

APRIL

All the 'stuff'' you don't like, help build a platform for future

success

REVIEW

What are your thoughts and feelings about this month?

What did you do this month for fun and inspiration?

Intentions and Goals

What are your intentions for the future?

What single task will take you one step closer to your dream?

OUTSTANDING TASKS

LIST OF POSSIBILITIES

Break out

of old habits

do

something

deliberately.

MAY

Even when you feel bad and life seems drab, don't give up!

Review

What are your thoughts and feelings about this month?

What did you do this month for fun and inspiration?

INTENTIONS AND GOALS

What are your intentions for the future?

What single task will take you one step closer to your dream?

OUTSTANDING TASKS

LIST OF POSSIBILITIES

What will you gain by giving up?

Have your ideas or your dream changed?

Do you want to be doing something else?

What new insights might you find when you try again?

JUNE

Don't compete. Your task is to be better than you were yesterday and be the best you can be, in what you choose to do

REVIEW

What are your thoughts and feelings about this month?

What did you do this month for fun and inspiration?

INTENTIONS AND GOALS

What are your intentions for the future?

What single task will take you one step closer to your dream?

OUTSTANDING TASKS

LIST OF POSSIBILITIES

When you wake up.... Get

up! Who knows what the day might bring, it could hold something special just for you. Treat it right.

Mid Year Review

Whatever you intended to accomplish this year is either well in-hand or taking shape. If you have not seen any changes that you consider progress, you may need to review the following:

- Your time frame for completion.

- Obstacles that may be hindering you.

- Whether you are still passionate about the idea and if your ardour has died what is the reason for that.

- Whether or not the goal you set is truly what you want.

- Is it really true there has been no progress or are you just giving yourself a hard time?

On the following pages looking specifically at what you thought did and did not work. Then with those ideas in mind, rewrite your outline plans for the rest of the year amending as you see fit.

ACCOMPLISHMENTS

Make a note of your accomplishments so far this year.

PROGRESSION

How do you feel about the year so far?

REVIEW YOUR PLANS

Make an outline for July to September.

JULY

AUGUST

SEPTEMBER

REVIEW YOUR PLANS

Make an outline for October to December.

OCTOBER

NOVEMBER

DECEMBER

NOTES

Focus on the present...

What you do today is more important than what you did yesterday or will do tomorrow.

Find a reason...
Do everything purposefully.

RECORD YOUR PROGRESS

JULY

Be observant!

REVIEW

What are your thoughts and feelings about this month?

What did you do this month for fun and inspiration?

NTENTIONS AND GOALS

What are your intentions for the future?

What single task will take you one step closer to your dream?

OUTSTANDING TASKS

LIST OF POSSIBILITIES

Get out of your way...

Let your light shine so you can see the path.

AUGUST

Your life itself is creativity in action. Why should you not be able to create something out of nothing?

REVIEW

What are your thoughts and feelings about this month?

What did you do this month for fun and inspiration?

INTENTIONS AND GOALS

What are your intentions for the future?

What single task will take you one step closer to your dream?

OUTSTANDING TASKS

LIST OF POSSIBILITIES

Approach

even the smallest task, with good intentions.

SEPTEMBER

You'll learn far more, about your abilities by taking action, than by merely trying to figure out all that could go wrong

REVIEW

What are your thoughts and feelings about this month?

What did you do this month for fun and inspiration?

Intentions and Goals

What are your intentions for the future?

What single task will take you one step closer to your dream?

September

OUTSTANDING TASKS

LIST OF POSSIBILITIES

There is motive behind everything

Just make sure yours fulfil the goals you're hoping to achieve!

OCTOBER

You cannot afford to wait until you are good at something before you do it

REVIEW

What are your thoughts and feelings about this month?

What did you do this month for fun and inspiration?

INTENTIONS AND GOALS

What are your intentions for the future?

What single task will take you one step closer to your dream?

OUTSTANDING TASKS

LIST OF POSSIBILITIES

This is your life. How you gonna live it?

NOVEMBER

It's the doing, being and becoming that makes you good

REVIEW

What are your thoughts and feelings about this month?

What did you do this month for fun and inspiration?

INTENTIONS AND GOALS

What are your intentions for the future?

What single task will take you one step closer to your dream?

OUTSTANDING TASKS

LIST OF POSSIBILITIES

Well?

DECEMBER

Change what doesn't work then try again

REVIEW

What are your thoughts and feelings about this month?

What did you do this month for fun and inspiration?

INTENTIONS AND GOALS

What are your intentions for the future?

What single task will take you one step closer to your dream?

December

OUTSTANDING TASKS

LIST OF POSSIBILITIES

Be mistress of your life!

FULL YEAR REVIEW

This is it, well done. Be proud of yourself. How can it get even better than this?

Did you make this year your most successful ever?

It is time yet again to reflect and make decisions. How do you feel now about your ability to create clear intentions and actually bring your ideas to life?

Did you accomplish what you set out to do?

Are you on the road to where you want to be?

Did you discover things about yourself you didn't know before?

Your task now is to be the best you can be at being you. Once more, appreciate everything that brought you here, the good, bad and the ugly. Remember that you did not arrive here on your efforts alone, your trials as well as the wonderful moments of success were created with the assistance of others.

ACCOMPLISHMENTS

Make a note of your accomplishments to date

FULL YEAR REVIEW

How do you feel about your accomplishments this year?

WHAT DID YOU LEARN?

What did you learn about yourself?

OTHER POSSIBILITIES

What would you do differently?

Take pleasure in watching as your ideas come alive!

NEXT YEAR

What infinite possibilities are held in the year ahead? What would you like to accomplish?

Date

....

AN OUTLINE FOR NEXT YEAR

Write freely about your intentions for next year.

JANUARY – FEBRUARY

Outline the months ahead by setting simple goals and tasks

JANUARY

FEBRUARY

MARCH - APRIL

Outline the months ahead by setting simple goals and tasks

MARCH

APRIL

M<small>AY</small> – J<small>UNE</small>

Outline the months ahead by setting simple goals and tasks

M<small>AY</small>

J<small>UNE</small>

July – August

Outline the months ahead by setting simple goals and tasks

July

August

September – October

Outline the months ahead by setting simple goals and tasks

SEPTEMBER

OCTOBER

November – December

Outline the months ahead by setting simple goals and tasks

NOVEMBER

DECEMBER

Make it happen

Success begins in your mind, moves to your hands, your body, then into your life. Continue to foster the belief in your ability to create something out of nothing. You are more than capable.

- Create an intention and set smart goals.

- Decide your measure of success.

- Write a plan.

- Take action.

- Make lists.

- Keep a journal.

- Stay committed.

- Have fun and be kind to yourself.

- Seek out progressive people with whom you can collaborate.

How can you make next year even better than this and really begin living the life of your dreams?

.

Notes

Notes

Notes

Notes

ADDITIONAL RESOURCES BY GWYNETH

This book is one of a series designed specifically for women, to assist you in living an authentically empowered life. Please see the following page for a list of accompanying books.

BOOKS

Why not purchase this book again or choose from the following

A Handbook of Grassroots Philosophy for Women	Written in a very easy to follow manner, this philosophical handbook offers wisdom, guidance and practical insight to aspects of life that are often the greatest stumbling blocks to creating lasting change.
Shaping Your Life from the Inside Out Workbook	Provides a systematic approach to transforming your life with self-affirming and practical exercises to create lasting change.
Plan Your Most Successful Year Ever	The personal success planner that guides you step-by-step to refining your goals, monitoring your progress and realising your dreams.
Plan Your Most Successful Year Planner Companion	This planner has less text and offers more planning pages. Are you about to start a new project? This will assist you in clarifying your aims focusing your ideas.
Life Goals	30 days to affirm and clarify your purpose and goals.
Looking Ahead to the Next 5 Years	Assists you in planning for a future that allows you to live how you choose, rather than a life led by circumstances alone.
The Gratitude Journal	60 days to change your mind and develop an attitude of gratitude.
This Day I Call Your Name	Little book of inspiration: poems and prayers. Poetic words to inspire, encourage, lift your spirits and brighten your day.
Notepads & Journals	Additional pages for creating lists, writing your reflections and journaling your progress. To bring your dreams to life.

FURTHER INFORMATION

www.planyouryear.com or www.successisyours.co.uk

RECEIVE 10% DISCOUNT

Register your interest in purchasing the accompanying workbook "Shaping Your Life from the Inside Out" and receive a 10% discount.

Send an email to books@successisyours.co.uk with the information below and in the Subject Line put: 'PYMSE - Shape Your Life Discount'

- First Name:
- Last Name:
- Email Address:
- Zip/Post Code:
- Contact Phone No:
- Keyword: Shape Your Life

Visit www.successisyours.co.uk to register for the Personal Success Newsletter and receive the free tip sheet "**5 Steps to Personal Success**"

www.ingramcontent.com/pod-product-compliance
Lightning Source LLC
Chambersburg PA
CBHW051504170526
45166CB00001B/380